D0603948

Presented to:

_____

Presented by:

_____

Date:

_____

For the Love of Dogs

A Delightful Photo Celebration of Life with Man's Best Friend

There is no psychiatrist in the world
like a puppy licking your face.

BERN WILLIAMS

Introduction

Fiercely loyal, totally faithful, and wanting nothing more than to be your personal companion—DOGS certainly fulfill the motto, "Man's Best Friend."

Of all the heartwarming attributes these canine friends exhibit, the greatest is…they simply love you! You would be hard-pressed to find a better example of unconditional love and devotion on this Earth.

For the Love of Dogs is a celebration of these furry companions in every shape and size. It is filled with humorous and heart-tugging photos that will make you smile and warm your heart.

At the end of the book there is even a special place for your own doggie photos and space for you to write your personal tribute about your own beloved friend.

So sit down and relax with your favorite canine and take a journey into all that is DOG. As you snuggle together, you'll be reminded of something you already knew—life has more meaning when shared with a faithful, furry friend.

There is beauty
in all God's creatures,
great and small…

But when God created the dog,

He created a loving masterpiece!

God designed this love
to come in all shapes,
sizes, and breeds.

Sometimes love even comes
gift-wrapped in fur…

And once you let a dog into your house
he always finds a way into your heart.

Yes, a dog is a beautiful thing.

To a dog, family always comes first…

Even though he understands
that close-knit families occasionally
step on one another's toes.

She may be small,
but she has a heart big enough
for a lifetime of love.

He always knows when you need
a kiss to make it all better…

Because you mean more to him
than food itself.

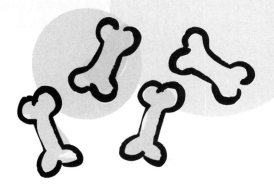

She will always be
your Valentine.

No matter how different you are,
he loves you…

And he will always be there
to give you a helping hand.

When you speak, she is all ears…

And she always
laughs at your jokes.

A dog always longs
for your return.

One thing for sure—
she sees you through the eyes of love.

And although your dog
may be a star…

When she has a bad hair day,
she just shakes it off.

A few wrinkles never
lower his self-esteem . . .

And he is perfectly comfortable being
exactly who God made him to be.

She never asks herself,
"If I eat this, will it go to my hips?"

And you can be sure that he never wastes
his days counting carbs.

She is
never concerned
over being seen in the
same outfit…

And while there may be copy cats in
this life, she reminds you
that everything God has created
is a bona fide original.

Cookie

He teaches you to dream
about the possibilities . . .

And shows you what being patient
is all about.

She reminds you that
sometimes big things
come in small packages.

She'll show you how to
be loyal to your friends . . .

And teach you how to hang on,
even when life is tough.

From him you'll learn
the "art of relaxing" . . .

Because he knows a power nap
can be a wonderful thing.

He'll snuggle with you under
the covers . . .

But when it's time to work,
he will be by your side.
No questions asked.

Although she sometimes can't help
but make a mess . . .

MARTIN

She puts on a brave face
and cleans up just fine!

He'll bring you the remote . . .

And he'll even groove to your music.

His favorite song?
"Born to be Wild!"

She'll let you play "dress up"…

And she'll even play
hide and seek.

He'll go with you anywhere . . .

And you'll always dine with a friend.

So—who is your dog?
He's really "Superdog" in disguise.

Dogs are just way cool!

What's not to love?

In Their Own Words
(What dogs would say if they could talk)

Dogs laugh, but they laugh with their tails.

MAX EASTMAN

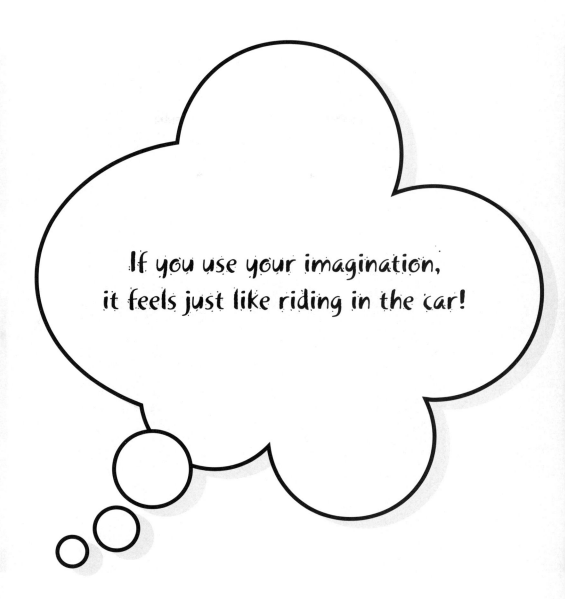

My Best Friend

Place your
dog's photo
here.

I love my dog because …

Always remember . . .
you'll never walk alone
when you have a dog.

Do you have funny or heart-tugging pictures of your treasured pet? We would love to consider your photos for future inspirational pet books.

We need photos that are:
· In digital format
· At least 4 X 5 and 300 dpi

Submitting photos:
· Please email your photos to: petphotos@bordonbooks.com
· In subject line, put your last name and species of pet.
· It is helpful if you send one photo at a time.
· Include your full name, address, and phone numbers with area code.
· If you would like, include a one-line caption for the photo.

When your photo is accepted:
· We will ask you to sign a release for non-exclusive rights to publish your photo.
· We will send you a complimentary copy of the book in which your photo appears.
· We will credit you by name for the photo.

Thanks for your interest; we look forward to receiving your delightful photos.

Please email your photo to petphotos@bordonbooks.com

If this book has touched your life, we would love to hear from you.
Please send your correspondence (no photos please) to:
Editorialdept@whitestonebooks.com
Visit our Web site at: www.whitestonebooks.com

WHITE STONE BOOKS
LAKELAND, FLORIDA